# How Kids Live
# Around the World

ALBATROS

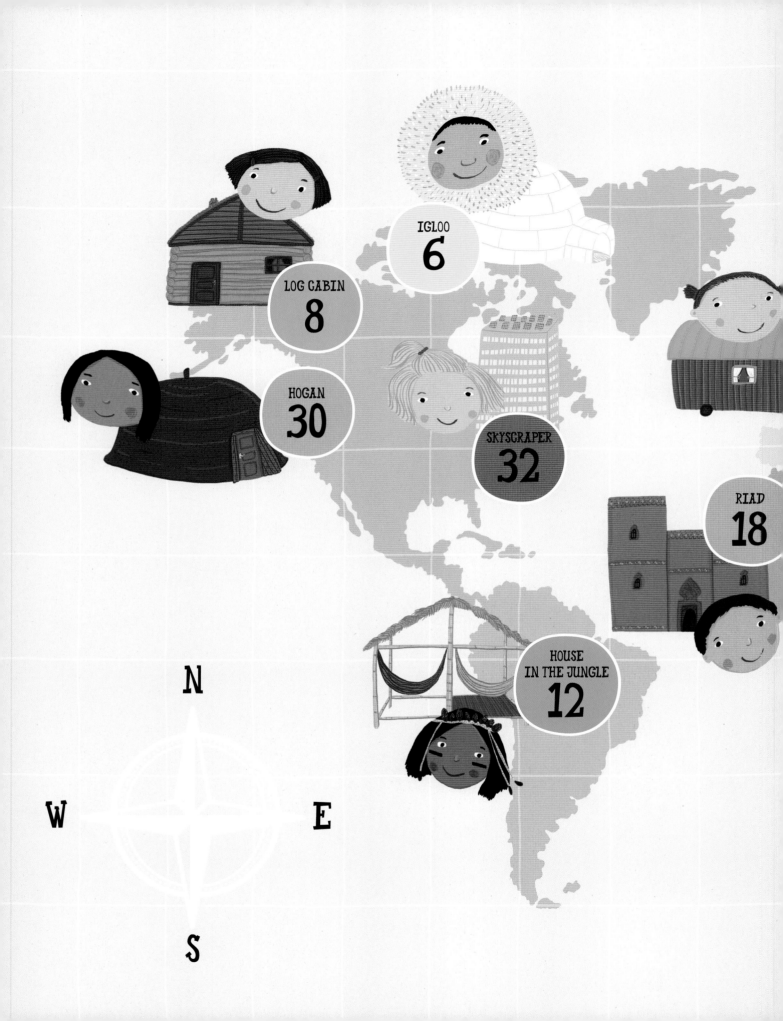

IGLOO
6

LOG CABIN
8

HOGAN
30

SKYSCRAPER
32

RIAD
18

HOUSE
IN THE JUNGLE
12

N

W

E

S

FARM
**26**

CARAVAN
**24**

CAVE
HOUSE
**28**

TENT IN
THE DESERT
**16**

YURT
**34**

HOUSE
ON STILTS
**10**

MACHIYA
**20**

HOUSEBOAT
**22**

COLORFUL
HOUSE
**14**

# Everyone lives somewhere

Children are the same the world over—they like to spend time with their family, play with friends, and have fun. But they learn different customs and become familiar with different environments, depending on where they live and grow up. This familiarization begins at home, as people build and arrange their homes according to where they live and which building materials are at hand. Some build with bricks, others with wood or stone, and some even use snow!

I live in a house on stilts.

This is our igloo.

Nice to meet you!

# Into the wind and rain

Nomadic peoples, such as the Mongols and the Bedouins, live in inhospitable climes, where travel is necessary for survival. Their homes are easy to dismantle and rebuild, meaning that they can take them on their travels. In places with an annual rainy season, people build homes that provide protection from heavy rain and floods. On the other hand, those who live in regions with very high summer temperatures design their homes to provide coolness and shade. And just think of the Inuit, who live in the land of eternal ice! They, too, have figured out over centuries how to build a home that suits their circumstances perfectly.

# There are all kinds of houses

Although many cultures continue to live in traditional dwellings, often it is impossible for them to manage without modern amenities. In comparison with some houses, others may appear a little sparse, but you should know that in most cases those who live in them don't mind this at all. The most important thing is to have the whole family together and enjoy shared moments. How else—apart from their building materials and facilities—can homes differ? Why, in size, of course! Some buildings are only big enough for one small family, and even then space is tight, while some huge ones—such as skyscrapers with over ninety floors—can house hundreds of families.

Bedouin tent

Have fun!

Moroccan riad

Circus acrobats live in a caravan!

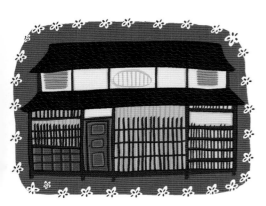

Welcome to our home!

5

# NANUQ lives in an igloo

**AI!** MY NAME'S **NANUQ**, AND I'M AN INUIT. I LIVE WITH MY MOM AND DAD IN A VILLAGE FAR BEYOND THE ARCTIC CIRCLE, WHERE THERE IS ICE AND SNOW ALL YEAR-ROUND. EVERY FAMILY IN OUR VILLAGE LIVES IN AN IGLOO—A LITTLE HOUSE BUILT OF SNOW, THE INSIDE OF WHICH IS LOVELY AND WARM IN SPITE OF THE HEAVY FROSTS. ALTHOUGH LIFE IN THE NORTH IS HARD, WE HAVE LOTS OF FUN HERE.

## 10 Vents

When building an igloo it's important to have enough air inside. For this reason special vents are drilled into the finished homes.

## 1 Canine companions

Since time immemorial we've been transported about by teams of dogs. Dogs also help us when we hunt, they protect us from predators, and we keep them as pets.

6

9

8

tunnel

5

fish

THIS IS
### NANUQ

## 2 Qulliq

We use a *qulliq* as a source of light, for cooking, for drying clothing, and in certain religious rituals. It is a soapstone lamp in which blubber is burned, with a piece of moss or grass used as a wick.

## 3 The Hunt

If we hadn't learned to hunt marine animals, we wouldn't have survived in the polar climate. Our hunters use traditional rods, harpoons, spears, arrows, and rifles too.

## 9 Snowmobiles

We use a snowmobile when traveling longer distances. For instance, we kids take a snowmobile to school.

## 8 Iggaak

Iggaak snow goggles protect our eyes from the fierce spring sunlight. They are made of bone or wood.

## 7 Winter Clothes

We wear very warm clothing made of animal skins. Parkas—traditional patterned coats with hoods—are popular. My mom sews skins together with a needle made of animal bone.

## 6 Villages

In the past, Inuit often had to move in search of food, so sometimes they had to disassemble their igloos and reassemble them in a new place. Today many have abandoned the nomadic way of life, and in villages we find houses made of wood, sheet metal, and stone.

animal skins

## 5 Igloo Construction

Igloos are built from big blocks of snow placed one on top of another in a circle. A short underground tunnel leads inside. On the far side of the igloo is a raised floor for us to sleep on.

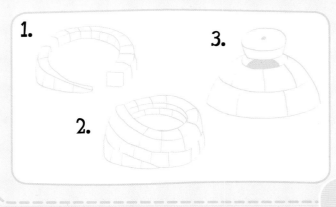

1.

2.

3.

## 4 Igloo Toilets

The children of Inuit families have one unpleasant chore—every day they have to carry from the igloo buckets that serve as toilets for those who live in the house!

# EMILY lives in a log cabin

HELLO! MY NAME'S **EMILY**, AND I COME FROM CANADA, WHERE MY PARENTS WORK AS PARK RANGERS AT A NATIONAL PARK. WE LIVE IN A LOG CABIN IN THE MIDDLE OF A FOREST, WITH A VIEW OF A MOUNTAIN RANGE AND A LARGE LAKE. THE NEAREST TOWN IS SEVERAL HOURS AWAY, BUT WE LIKE MEETING CAMPERS VISITING THE PARK.

## 1 Electricity

In the past, people in the middle of the wilderness had only their own strength to rely on. Today we're able to use electrical appliances. In our cellar we have a generator, which allows us to produce our own electricity.

## 2 Thatched roof

The roof of our log cabin is covered with grass and moss. Thanks to this, it's warm inside—even in winter. The thatch provides better protection from rain and snow than the wood itself.

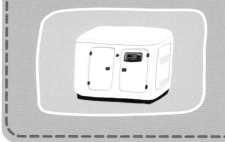

## 10 Axes and saws

Although it's sometimes necessary to cut down a tree, it's important to maintain nature's balance in the forest by not felling too many trees.

cellar

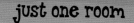

just one room

## 3 Just one room

These days luxury log cabins are built for tourists, but ours is the traditional type, with just one room, where we sleep, cook, talk, and work. Only the bathroom is in a separate room.

## 9 All made of wood

Log cabins are built from tree trunks sawed and stripped of bark—as this is the material most readily available. The individual logs are clearly visible inside as well, and this makes the home cosy. The furniture, too, is made of wood.

## 8 Pails of water

Our drinking water comes from a deep well near the cabin. Fortunately, our plumbing is connected to it—that way, we don't have to carry water inside in pails like they did in the olden days!

## 7 Spectacular view

Our log cabin is in the middle of a forest, so me and my parents really enjoy nature walks. We often go to the lake, where we enjoy the peace and quiet—and above all, the spectacular view!

## 6 Snowed under

Winter snowfall is sometimes so heavy that we have to use a large snow shovel to dig our way out of our cabin!

## 5 Warmth first

Canadian winters are very cold, and the summers are cooler, too—the temperature can fall below the freezing point. For this reason there's a fireplace in my family's cabin, and we always have enough logs to heat with.

## 4 Homeschooling

As we live a long way away from school, instead of commuting daily, I do homeschooling with my parents. They are as strict with me as teachers at school would be—they even give me extra homework.

grass and moss

THIS IS EMILY

# LAMON lives in a house on stilts

**SAWASDEE!** I'M **LAMON**, AND I LIVE IN THAILAND, WHERE EVERY SUMMER THERE IS A RAINY SEASON. AS OUR VILLAGE IS NEAR A RIVER THAT REGULARLY BURSTS ITS BANKS, OUR HOUSE STANDS ON HIGH STILTS, AND WE GET INSIDE BY CLIMBING A LADDER. THIS WAY WE CAN ALWAYS STAY DRY. THE GROUND FLOOR PROVIDES SHELTER FROM THE HEAT OF THE SUN.

## 1 Houses on stilts

Not only do the wooden stilts our houses are built on protect us from flooding and provide shade, but they also prevent livestock from entering the home. Some people have a workshop or a store between the stilts.

## 2 Sloping roof

Our houses have very steep roofs—in the rainy season the slope diverts water to the ground, stopping it from leaking into the house.

## 3 A river like a street

Our village lies on both banks of the river on which our lively street life takes place. Not only do boats serve as transport, but market vendors offering interesting wares also have their stalls on them.

## 10 Fruit

There's never a shortage of fruit in Thailand. Throughout the day we like to eat coconuts, bananas, mangoes, pineapples, pomelos, lychees, and other fruits.

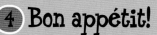

THIS IS
**LAMON**

## 4 Bon appétit!

Our staple food is rice, which is served in special rice baskets. We also like to cook meat on skewers, as well as noodles soups, and hot sauces. We eat with our hands, seated on the floor.

## 9 Beauty in simplicity

You won't find much furniture inside our houses—we like lots of space. Besides, we often live in multi-generational households. Although we don't have a lot of privacy, we have a lot of fun.

## 8 Spirit house

At home we have a little decorated altar dedicated to local good spirits; here we lay small offerings to ensure that the spirits in the house are happy.

the kitchen

## 7 Life on the porch

We like to spend a lot of time on the porch that adjoins our house. Here we play with our friends, talk together, and eat.

a market vendor

## 6 Hats

We protect ourselves from the sun by wearing bamboo hats. Some of these, such as the flat-topped *ngob*, let in a flow of air to keep our heads cool.

## 5 Barefoot

It is our custom to go barefoot at home, even in the temple. We take off our shoes at the entrance to a building.

# YARA lives in a house in the jungle

**TAPEIKO PORÃ!** MY NAME'S **YARA**, AND I LIVE IN THE AMAZON RAINFOREST. TODAY ABOUT 1 MILLION INDIGENOUS INHABITANTS LIKE ME LIVE IN AMAZONIA, IN ABOUT 400 TRIBES. ALTHOUGH MOST OF US NOW KNOW ABOUT LARGE MODERN CITIES, WE PREFER TO STAY AT HOME, IN THE PLACE WHERE OUR ANCESTORS LIVED—THE PRIMEVAL FOREST. IT PROVIDES FOR ALL OUR NEEDS, AND WE DO OUR BEST TO PROTECT IT.

## 10 Hammocks

In our huts we sleep not on the ground but in hammocks. Mothers rock their babies in them, too.

## 1 Our riverside village

We live by the riverbank, and we travel great distances in canoes. It would take us much longer to journey the same distance through the jungle, and it would be more dangerous.

## 2 Fishing with poison

We fish by throwing poisoned bait into the water and waiting for the fish to swallow it. When they swim up to the surface in a daze, we can catch them easily.

## 3 Blowpipes

Our men are skilled hunters. They hunt with blowpipes, from which they shoot arrows tipped with a poison called *curare*.

## 4 Climbing for honey

We love the taste of wild honey. Brave adults are able to climb to bees' nests using ropes made of leaves, which they knot loosely around the tree.

hammock

## 9 After work comes fun

After work we still have time for amusement. We often go on visits and hold celebrations. We also use natural materials to make things including jewelry, weapons, toys, and clothing.

## 8 Our diet

Every day the women go work in the fields, cultivating maize, cassava, beans, and bananas. We children gather nuts, clams, and grubs, which are considered delicacies.

## 7 Shamans

We believe that every being, plant, and stone has its own spirit. But some spirits are evil and can cause us various problems. These spirits are appeased by shamans, who perform rituals in order to speak with them.

honeycombs

THIS IS YARA

## 5 Great knowledge of flora & fauna

From a young age we get to know the jungle like the back of our hand. Otherwise we'd be at risk of eating a poisonous plant or disturbing the sleep of a dangerous predator.

## 6 Monkey business

My father found this little monkey abandoned in the jungle. Now it's my faithful friend.

# MZAMO lives in a colorful house

**EE YEBO!** MY NAME'S **MZAMO**, AND I'M A MEMBER OF SOUTH AFRICA'S NDEBELE PEOPLE. I LIVE WITH MY FAMILY IN A LITTLE HOUSE, PLUS TWO SMALL HUTS THAT CONTAIN THE KITCHEN AND THE GRANARY. OUR HOMESTEAD CONTAINS A COURTYARD, WHICH IS SURROUNDED BY A LOW WALL. LOOK HOW LOVELY AND COLORFUL ALL OUR BUILDINGS ARE!

## 10 Sleeping mats

At home we sleep on the ground. We all have our own mat, which protects us from the cold and keeps us comfortable.

## 1 Wall around a house

Our homestead comprises the main house, the kitchen, and the granary. These are surrounded by a decorated wall, which prevents livestock from coming into our courtyard.

## 2 Feminine beauty

We Ndebele are famous for jewelry made from colored glass beads and for the copper rings the women wear around their necks. Women here are adorned with many rings, necklaces, and headdresses, worn all at the same time.

kitchen

## 3 House-building

Although men and women work together to build a house, the final plastering—with a mix of clay and cow dung—is a job for women only. As soon as the plaster has been dried by the sun, the women set to decorating it.

## 4 Traditional division of labor

The work of men and women is traditionally divided. Men take care of the livestock and fields, and they build whatever is needed. Women look after the home and make jewelry, baskets, and mats.

14

## 9 Colored symbols

Following tradition, we decorate our homes with colorful geometric patterns. These have a number of different meanings—some even look like televisions or razors!

## 8 Initiation ceremony

In puberty, boys and girls undergo a procedure of initiation. The girl's ceremony takes place at home and lasts a week, but boys have to attend an initiation school for two whole months.

## 7 Cross

Although today many of us are Christians who go to church regularly, we keep a lot of very old traditions.

granary

THIS IS
MZAMO

## 5 Livestock everywhere

We keep a small herd of goats and sheep. The hens that run around provide us with eggs.

## 6 School every day

My friends and I walk a long way to school, where we learn to read, write, and count, and we learn about history and how to speak foreign languages. We also wear uniforms at school.

# DIHYA lives in a tent in the desert

MAR HABA! MY NAME'S **DIHYA**, AND I'M ONE OF THE BEDOUIN NOMADS WHO LIVE IN THE SAHARA. SEVERAL FAMILIES LIVE TOGETHER, MOVING TOGETHER FROM PLACE TO PLACE. THAT'S WHY I DON'T GO TO SCHOOL; INSTEAD I HELP MY MOM LOOK AFTER MY BROTHERS AND SISTERS, THE HOUSEHOLD, AND OUR LIVESTOCK. ALTHOUGH LIFE IN THE DESERT ISN'T EASY, I WOULDN'T TRADE IT FOR THE WORLD!

## 10 Baking bread

To make our flatbread we use a special convex baking tray, which we heat over a fire.

## 1 Building a tent

As our tent is light and easy to store, it can be put up quickly. Besides the tent, all we need are a few carpets, some wooden stakes, ropes, and woven fabrics. We don't have many things in our tent, so as to make our homes easier to carry.

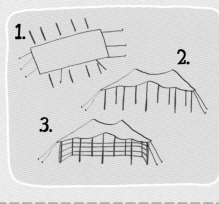

## 2 Water

As water is scarce in the desert, it is very valuable to us. We find it at oases—small lakes in the desert surrounded by some greenery. We store water in barrels or other containers, and we use it to make the tea that we drink throughout the day.

## 3 Figs

We can buy or sell various wares at markets that are held at oases. We personally have some lovely sweet figs to sell!

## 4 Carpet weaving

We're able to weave beautiful carpets from camel hair. We decorate our tents with these or sell them to tourists.

## 9 Turbans & barracans

In the desert it's not advisable to expose your skin to the sun, as it will burn quickly. So we cover ourselves in long coats known as *barracans* and wear turbans or scarves on our heads.

## 8 Musical instruments

After a busy day, in the evening we like to relax. Often we sing our songs, accompanying ourselves on traditional drums, flutes, and stringed instruments.

## 7 Danger

A lot of dangerous creatures, like scorpions, live in the desert. The smaller the scorpion, the more poisonous it is!

## 6 Not just sand

Don't get the idea that the Sahara is nothing but sand! There are also hills, grasslands, and temporary rivers called *wadis*. Without these, we'd have no water and the animals would have nothing to eat.

THIS IS **DIHYA**

## 5 Camels & goats

As we rarely get to villages or towns, we keep various animals, which provide us with food, materials, and even companionship!

# ABDUL lives in a riad

**SALAM!** MY NAME'S **ABDUL**. WELCOME TO OUR HOME! I LIVE WITH MY SISTER AND PARENTS IN A TRADITIONAL MOROCCAN HOUSE CALLED A RIAD, WHICH EXTENDS RIGHT AROUND OUR COURTYARD AND GARDEN. THIS PROVIDES US WITH PRIVACY, PROTECTION, AND QUIET. MANY RIADS TODAY SERVE AS HOTELS FOR TOURISTS.

## 10 Tea

We drink our famous green tea with mint all year long. In summer when it's hot, our mom makes it into ice tea.

## 1 Life on the roof

On the roof of our house there's a terrace where we can relax in the evening. As the terrace is warmed by the sun, we can sit on it even when it's cool outside.

THIS IS **ABDUL**

## 2 Satellite dish

Although we live in an old house, that doesn't mean that we don't have TV or the internet at home!

## 3 Fountain

Every garden must have a fountain, which serves as a natural air-conditioner. The water cools the warm air that flows in through the open roof.

## 4 Garden inside the house

We approach our house through an entrance that leads into the courtyard and garden. I enjoy helping with the gardening.

## 9 Neighbors

It's easy for us to visit other children in the neighborhood. We just go out onto the roof terrace and cross over to the next house!

## 8 The Koran

Many of the inscriptions we decorate our walls with are quotations from the Koran. We're Muslims, so for us the Koran is our holy book, as the Bible is for Christians.

## 7 Lemon trees

There are four lemon trees in our garden. Not only do these provide us with our own lemons, but we can also relax in their shade.

## 6 Ornamentation

To make our house prettier still, we decorate the walls with colored mosaic tiles and ornamental inscriptions in Arabic.

## 5 Only small windows?

The windows facing the street are small and unremarkable, while those with a view of the garden are large. This arrangement gives our home greater privacy.

# MIYUKI lives in a machiya

**KONNICHI WA!** MY NAME'S **MIYUKI**, AND I LIVE WITH MY PARENTS IN A MACHIYA, A TRADITIONAL JAPANESE WOODEN HOUSE WITH A SMALL SHOP ON THE GROUND FLOOR. THE HOUSE IS DIVIDED INTO SEVERAL PARTS, FOR LIVING IN AND FOR DOING BUSINESS IN. THERE ARE SEVERAL SUCH HOUSES IN OUR NEIGHBORHOOD, AND WE GET ALONG VERY WELL WITH OUR NEAREST NEIGHBORS. WHEN MY HOMEWORK ALLOWS, AFTER SCHOOL I HELP MY PARENTS IN THE COFFEE SHOP.

## 11 Genkan

Before we enter the house, we must take off our shoes. Our house has a special entryway for this, called a *genkan*.

## 1 Shop on the ground floor

Machiyas face the street. Often they have a narrow shop at the front and living space that stretches a long way back. In our house my parents have set up a coffee shop.

THIS IS **MIYUKI**

## 2 Kamidana

As Shintoists, we worship spirits called *kami*, and this is what the *kamidana* altar is for. It must contain a 'house' and various objects for the kami.

## 3 Shoji

Rooms are divided by sliding doors and windows, called *shoji*. These are made of rice paper over frames of bamboo.

## 4 Rice

In the past the front part of a house served as a shop selling silk or rice. Rice forms the basis of Japanese cuisine to this day.

## 10 Futon

My futon bed is easy to fold and store away, as it comprises only mattresses and quilts. So it doesn't take up space in my room unnecessarily!

## 9 Tatami

In the past, tatami mats were used instead of carpets. These days we prefer wooden flooring and have tatami only in the traditional room.

## 8 Garden

There is a secret place inside our house—the garden, which is decorated with rockeries and bonsai. This is where we go to relax and enjoy a bit of nature.

## 7 Tokonoma

In the living room there is an alcove called a *tokonoma*, which contains decorative objects. We like to give our guests a pleasant view of this alcove, which no one should enter without good reason—there is something a little sacred about it.

## 5 Kotatsu

As we don't have central heating, in winter we use a low wooden table called a *kotatsu*, which has a built-in electric heater. This is covered with a blanket, which holds in the warmth. We sit around this to talk, have dinner, or play games together.

## 6 Washitsu

In the past, the *washitsu*, a traditional Japanese room, was used as a bedroom. These days it tends to be a decorative room, always containing tatami mats, shoji doors and windows, and Japanese ornaments and furniture.

# HARAN lives on a houseboat

**NAMASTE.** AND WELCOME TO INDIA! MY NAME'S **HARAN**, AND I LIVE WITH MY FAMILY BY A LAKE IN THE STATE OF KERALA. MOST OF THE TIME WE LIVE IN A LITTLE HOUSE, BUT DURING THE TOURIST SEASON WE SPEND OUR DAYS ON THE HOUSEBOAT, WHERE MY DAD WORKS AS A GUIDE. WHEN I'M NOT AT SCHOOL, I HELP HIM ON THE BOAT. WE CATCH FISH TOGETHER AND LOOK AFTER THE BOAT AND THE TOURISTS.

## 10 What is a houseboat?

A houseboat is a boat designed to be used as a home and to transport cargo. These days it is used mainly for tourism. From our houseboat, people can get to know the nature and life of South India.

## 1 Hindu altar

An important part of our boat is the small altar where we pray for health and happiness. Like most Indians, we are Hindus, so we have many gods to turn to.

## 2 No nails

The construction of an Indian houseboat is unique, as it uses not a single nail. It is built of planks of wood held together by ropes made of coconut fiber. We use only local materials, so our boats are good for the environment.

## 3 School

I love helping my dad, but I have to go to school, too. It's easy to get there—by boat!

## 9 Tourists

Tourists come from all over the world to enjoy the natural beauty of our river and its surroundings. Dad and I try to ensure that they have a really good time on our houseboat and will take home fond memories of India.

## 8 Life buoys and life jackets

There are lots of life buoys and life jackets inside the boat. In case there's an accident, everyone would be able to swim ashore safely.

## 7 Fire towards the rear

We can cook on our boat, too. We make tasty Indian meals for ourselves and the tourists. We cook using coconut oil, as we have no shortage of coconut trees here!

THIS IS
HARAN

## 6 Mosquito nets

We need mosquito nets around our beds. Huge amounts of mosquitoes live by the water. Without the nets, they would bite us from head to toe while we sleep.

## 4 Fish oil and cashew oil

When a boat is almost finished, it is varnished, inside and out, with fish oil and cashew oil. This helps it stay in good condition for many years.

## 5 Slow pace of life

In order to carry huge loads, the boats must be huge, too! Because they move slowly with cargos of up to 30 tons—about the same weight as ten African elephants!—trips can take quite a long time.

23

# CLARA lives in a caravan

**HI!** I'M **CLARA**, AND I LIVE IN A CARAVAN, WHICH CAN EASILY BE STRAPPED TO OUR CAR AND DRIVEN TO A NEW PLACE. MY FAMILY RUNS A CIRCUS, WHICH WE TAKE AROUND THE WORLD. MY DAD IS THE RINGMASTER, WHICH MEANS THAT HE'S IN CHARGE OF EVERYTHING. MY BROTHER AND I HAVE BEEN PART OF THE CIRCUS SINCE WE WERE SMALL. ON OUR TRAVELS WE TRAIN FOR OUR SHOWS AND HELP OUR PARENTS.

## 10 Room on rails

If you think there's not much space in a caravan, you're mistaken! Some of our rooms can be extended, because they are built on telescopic rails.

## 1 Family of acrobats

Circus crafts are passed down from parent to child. My brother is an acrobat, and I know how to juggle. Dad thinks up all parts of our act and helps us practice them.

THIS IS **CLARA**

## 2 Amazing show

In the past, circuses always had to have animal acts. But in our circus there are only acrobats and artists, as we want animals to live happy lives, outside of captivity, in a natural environment.

## 3 Semi-nomadic life

Every week we travel to a different town and perform there. We live in a circus camp with a big top and caravans, where we rehearse our shows. Only in winter do we spend three months in one place, so that we can rest.

## 9 Tools

When we're traveling, we don't have much time. Every family carries tools so that if something goes wrong, we can mend our caravans ourselves.

## 8 Foreign-language dictionaries

Our shows take us to all corners of the world. It's good to know several languages so that we can give a proper welcome to our visitors in different countries.

## 7 Computer with internet

Our caravan is supplied with electricity, so we have all modern conveniences! I need a computer with internet for my schoolwork. Although Mom teaches us at home, we use the internet to complete tasks sent to us by a teacher at our school. Occasionally we go to school to take exams.

Clara's brother

## 6 Big top

The big top is a huge, colorful canvas that covers a circus tent. It's quite hard work to put it up and maintain it.

## 4 Modern kitchen

In our caravan there's a modern kitchen, too, where Mom does the cooking. We have a fridge, a dishwasher, and a microwave—unlike our grandparents, who cooked on an open fire outside.

## 5 Showers on wheels

Our caravan even contains a fully-functional bathroom and toilet. We don't need to be connected to the sewer system—we carry plenty of water with us, and from time to time we clean our toilets in designated places.

# PAUL lives on a farm

**GUTEN TAG!** MY NAME'S **PAUL**, AND I LIVE WITH MY FAMILY ON A FARM IN THE GERMAN COUNTRYSIDE. THERE'S ALWAYS LOTS TO DO ON A FARM, SO I HELP MY PARENTS WHENEVER I CAN. I LOOK AFTER THE ANIMALS, HELP IN THE SHOP, AND KEEP AN EYE ON MY YOUNGER SISTER.

## 10 Oven

We keep ourselves warm in winter by heating the oven. We use it for cooking and baking, too. Mom's homemade bread and cakes are fantastic!

## 1 Out of bed at six

We rise early so that we can manage all the work. All the animals need to be fed and the cows milked, and we have to tend the fields and let the animals out to pasture. My parents don't finish their work until late in the evening.

## 2 Churning butter

From cow's milk we make cheese, cream, and butter, which Mom churns in a wooden container. These are absolutely delicious!

tractor

## 3 Baby in a basket

Recently my little sister was born. To keep an eye on her at all times, Mom lays her in a basket, which she lulls her to sleep in, too.

## 4 Taking care of animals

All the animals we keep give us something—meat and milk from the cows, wool from the sheep. In return we give them good day-to-day care.

## 9 It doesn't matter that I get dirty

It's easy to get dirty when you're working on a farm, and I don't mind it at all. The main thing is, the animals are happy.

## 8 Shop

Our farm produces more food than we can eat. In our shop we sell eggs and dairy and meat products to tourists.

## 7 The henhouse

My family keeps a lot of hens, so Dad and I built them a henhouse, where they sleep at night. Here, too, they lay their eggs, which we collect in the morning.

THIS IS
PAUL

## 5 Lambs, baby goats, and calves

Animals are often born on our farm. Then in our pasture we see lambs, baby goats, and calves keeping close to their moms and learning everything important from them.

## 6 The rabbit hutch

We have rabbits, too, which we keep in a hutch. Every day I give them fresh water, hay, and plants from the meadow.

27

# TALYA lives in a cave house

MERHABA! MY NAME'S TALYA, AND I LIVE IN A PART OF TURKEY CALLED CAPPADOCIA. A LONG TIME AGO PEOPLE DUG OUT DWELLINGS IN THE JAGGED ROCKS HERE, TO PROVIDE REFUGE FROM THEIR ENEMIES. THE ENEMIES WENT AWAY, BUT PEOPLE CONTINUED TO LIVE IN THEIR CAVE HOUSES. ONLY TOURISTS STAY IN CAVE VILLAGES TODAY, BUT WHERE I COME FROM THERE ARE STILL A FEW FAMILIES WHO LIVE IN THE ROCKS. MINE, FOR INSTANCE.

## 1 Rooms dug into the rocks

Some single-story houses here look like ordinary houses. Others, though, are carved deep into the rock, even reaching underground. Most rooms have arched ceilings, to help the walls support the roof.

## 2 Hidden maze

From time to time one of our neighbors discovers a hidden entrance, leading from their house to a long-abandoned underground town that is hundreds of years old.

## 10 Doves

There are lots of bird houses carved into the rock. It's traditional for us to use dove droppings as fertilizer.

arched ceiling

## 3 Stoves

While the summers here are really hot, the winters are very cool. In winter we heat our houses with small stoves.

## 9 Paintings hundreds of years old

When our ancestors built the system of corridors and halls in the rock, they though it out really well. As well as corridors and halls, there were underground prayer rooms and storerooms. Some towns had eight underground floors! And in the local cave churches you can see paintings that are hundreds of years old.

## 8 Kebab

My favorite meal is *kebab*, a local speciality. It consists of meat, vegetables, and spices roasted in an oven in a ceramic container. This pot is cracked open before each meal is served. Kebab is super delicious!

## 7 Jagged rocks

The place where we live used to be a volcanic area, and its jagged rocks were formed by nature over thousands of years. Once people realized that these rocks could be hollowed out, they began to build their homes in them.

## 6 Supporting columns

As the rocks are quite old, they were recently fitted with supporting columns to keep us safe.

## 5 Traditional ceramics

Pots have been produced here for many centuries. They are beautifully decorated, and there are many different patterns to choose from.

bird house

THIS IS
TALYA

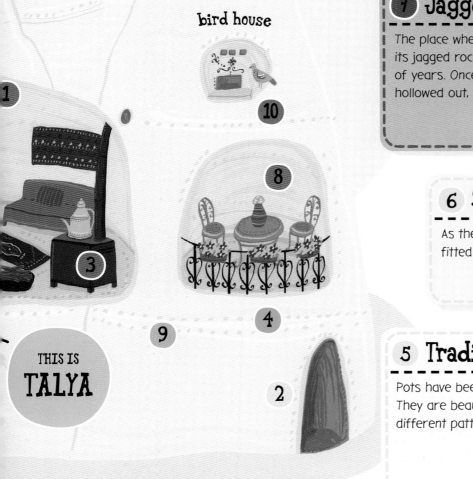

## 4 Terrace in the rock

As the rock is so easily shaped, our ancestors even dug terraces into it, where we can relax in the shade.

# GAD lives in a hogan

**YÁ'ÁT'ÉÉH!** MY NAME'S **GAD**, AND MY FAMILY IS PART OF THE NATIVE AMERICAN NAVAJO TRIBE. NATIVE AMERICANS ARE INDIGENOUS PEOPLE FROM AMERICA. AFTER CHRISTOPHER COLUMBUS ARRIVED IN AMERICA IN 1492, PEOPLE FROM ALL OVER THE WORLD BEGAN TO MOVE HERE, AND NATIVE AMERICANS GRADUALLY BECAME A MINORITY. TODAY THERE ARE FAR FEWER OF US THAN THERE USED TO BE, AND MANY OF US LIVE ON RESERVATIONS.

## 10 Frybread

Fried flatbread is a traditional Navajo food that can be eaten on its own. It is served savory or sweet.

## 1 Hogan

A hogan is a wooden building with a clay roof. There's not much room in it, but inside it is beautifully decorated with carpets. Today, however, most Native Americans live in modern houses, and hogans are used only for religious and festive occasions.

## 2 Traditional dress

In the past we wore ornate clothing made of animal skins or cotton, and leather shoes called moccasins. Today we dress as others do, wearing traditional clothing only on important occasions and for celebrations, when we dance in it.

## 3 Native American Reservations

Most people imagine that Native Americans, or Indians as we were once known, live in tepees. In actual fact we live in houses on reservations, which are more like small territories than villages.

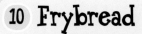

## 9 Going to the healer

When we are ill or injured, we go to the *hataali*, our healer. Having found out what is wrong with us, he treats us with a magical rite, prayer, and herbal medicines.

## 8 Comb

Our hair is very important to us, as it reflects our culture and values. We take great care of it. Usually we cut our hair short only when we are in mourning.

THIS IS GAD

## 7 School bus

As some of the houses on the reservation are far apart, we couldn't manage without our school bus, which stops at each house before driving us to school.

## 6 Loom

The Navajo Tribe is renowned for its skillful weavers of carpets and other textiles. These have geometric patterns and are beautifully colorful.

## 4 Horses

Horses were brought to America by the Spanish, which is how they reached us. In the past we used horses for transportation and for hunting buffalo. We remain very proud of our horses and do our best to protect them.

## 5 Maize, squashes, and beans

Native Americans have lived off the land since time immemorial. Our most important crops include maize, beans, and squashes. These provide us with food all year-round.

# OLIVIA lives in a skyscraper

**HEY THERE!** MY NAME'S **OLIVIA**, AND I LIVE WITH MY PARENTS IN A SKYSCRAPER IN NEW YORK CITY, WHICH IS HOME TO SO MANY PEOPLE THAT NOT EVERY FAMILY CAN HAVE ITS OWN HOUSE. SO THERE ARE LOTS OF SKYSCRAPERS—ENORMOUSLY TALL BUILDINGS WITH MANY PEOPLE LIVING IN THEM. THE TALLEST OF THESE HAVE OVER 90 FLOORS!

## 10 Fireplace

We can't have a real fireplace in our apartment because there's nowhere to put a chimney. So we have an electric fire that looks a lot like a real one—and is completely safe!.

## 1 Dependent on the elevator

As skyscrapers have lots of floors, we use the elevator to reach our apartment quickly. It would take a really long time to reach the fortieth floor by walking up the stairs!

## 2 Flower boxes

Some apartments have balconies, which are decorated with boxes for growing flowers and vegetables. As we don't have a garden, this is one way for us to be in touch with nature.

THIS IS
OLIVIA

## 3 Bird's eye view

As we live really high off the ground, from our apartment we can see the whole city—just as birds can. Although we live downtown, it's quiet here because we're so high up.

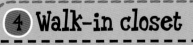

## 4 Walk-in closet

Although our apartment isn't very large, like most New Yorkers we have a walk-in closet!

## 9 Building reception

Every skyscraper has a reception desk and elevators on the ground floor. The receptionist knows the people who live in the house, takes care of their mail, supervises security, and makes sure that order is maintained in the building.

## 8 Fire-resistant walls and doors

Many people worry that in the event of a fire they wouldn't be able to get out of the skyscraper in time. But today's skyscrapers are built so as to minimize such a risk. It goes without saying that we have fire-resistant walls and doors, a sprinkler system, and emergency staircases.

## 7 Solar panels

A building as huge as a skyscraper uses a lot of energy. So people try to be kind to nature by installing solar roof panels, which generate some of their energy.

## 6 Spin dryer

Every apartment has a spin dryer, in which just-washed clothes dry very quickly.

## 5 Washing the windows

The windows of skyscrapers are washed only by specially trained workers, as at such a great height this is a dangerous job. Each worker has their own bucket of water and squeegee, and they wash each window by hand.

# BATU lives in a yurt

**SAIN BAINA UU!** MY NAME'S **BATU**, AND I LIVE WITH MY PARENTS, BROTHERS, AND SISTERS IN A TRADITIONAL MONGOLIAN DWELLING CALLED A YURT. WE MOVE FROM PLACE TO PLACE, SEVERAL TIMES A YEAR. A YURT IS A SUITABLE HOME FOR THE NOMADIC LIFE, AS IT IS EASY TO PACK AND SET UP IN DIFFERENT PLACES. A YURT MAKES AN ENORMOUS ROOM, WHERE WE CAN ALL BE TOGETHER. IN SUMMER, WHEN WE DON'T GO TO SCHOOL, WE HELP OUR PARENTS LOOK AFTER OUR ANIMALS.

## 10 Felt

The yurt's felt covering is made by the women. It protects our home from bad weather on the steppes. Often ornate carpets, too, are made of felt.

## 1 Motorcycle

Today's yurts contain many modern inventions, such as radios and televisions. While nomads used to ride horses when guarding their grazing livestock, now they tend to use motorcycles.

## 2 Building a yurt

A yurt is made of a lightweight wooden structure and a felt covering. During construction, the lattice wall sections are the first to be made tense. Then the door frame and the wheel at the center, to which the roof struts are connected, are installed. Finally the yurt is covered with several layers of felt, to keep it warm inside.

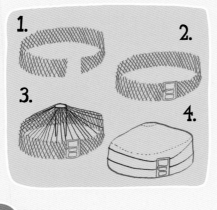

1.
2.
3.
4.

## 3 Yaks

The yak is one of five animal species that we most commonly keep. Yaks are very important to us, as all year-round they provide us with milk, meat, leather, and fur, which we use for making rope.

althar

## 9 Plains & steppes

Our landscape consists of plains and steppes, where nothing grows but grass. There are no trees or other woody plants here—the winds are too strong. A yurt's design ensures that it provides sufficient protection.

## 8 School

We start school when we're eight, and we study many different subjects. Some of my friends from nomadic families don't often go to school, though, as they have to help their parents.

## 7 Sacks and trunks

Our beautifully painted trunks are placed level with the sides of the yurt. We use these and sacks instead of large pieces of furniture, as they are easier to transport on our frequent moves.

THIS IS **BATU**

airag

## 6 Fireplace

In the middle of the yurt is a fireplace, where we cook and which we use to heat the tent. The smoke escapes through an opening in the roof.

## 4 Buddhist symbols in a yurt

We practice the Buddhist religion, and our homes are decorated with symbols that reflect our beliefs. These include the endless knot and the dharma wheel, which is depicted in the ring at the crown of the yurt.

## 5 Horse milk

Horse milk is used to make a drink called *airag*, which is so popular that it's considered to be Mongolia's national drink!

**How Kids Live Around the World**
Authors: Helena Haraštová, Pavla Hanáčková
Illustrator: Michaela Bergmannová

© Designed by B4U Publishing for Albatros,
an imprint of Albatros Media Group, 2021.
Na Pankráci 30, Prague 4, Czech Republic.
Printed in China by Leo Paper Group.
ISBN: 978-80-00-06129-0

www.albatrosbooks.com